AFFILIATE MARKETING FOR NEWBIES

HOW TO MAKE YOUR FIRST $1000 ONLINE
WITH NO EXPERIENCE

I0426989

John William

1

ISBN: 9798878110501

Printed in the United States of America

Table of Contents

Chapter 1
$1,000 In 30 Days Broken Down

Over the past 10 years I've made passive and consistent income online. There's nothing like waking up to money from work you did once that pays you over and over again. Once you get to the point where your passive income pays all of your bills – you are truly wealthy. Let us not get too far ahead of ourselves though, because I want to make something very clear here. The goal is not to get rich quick, rather I want you to focus on setting up a system right the first time so that you can experience your first $1,000 online. Now lets break that down. $1,000 divided by a 30 day time period is only $33.33 per day, and if you can build a system that averages $33.33 per day, congratulations you just made your first $1,000 online. Now it's time to scale, but for now - let's focus on placing your bricks down as perfectly as bricks can be laid, so that one day you will have a wall.

If you currently have a job, but the income you earn from it is not enough to fund most of the activities you are interested in taking part in, such as investment and saving. In such cases, it would be a good idea for you to get involved in a way of making money on your own terms, so that you don't need to quit your current job or conform to a regular schedule in order to get it done. If you are interested in doing this, you will find that doing affiliate marketing can turn out to be the best way to proceed. Why? Because it's very cheap to get started, there is no inventory, no customer service and no product fulfillment. All you're basically doing is referring people to a product or service, and when that occurs you'll get a commission. Think about how many times you referred someone to a restaurant, or a certain movie you enjoyed with your family, but didn't get paid for it. Now it's time to set up a system and do what you are already doing except this time you'll get a piece of the pie.

How Does It Work?

In a nutshell, affiliate marketing is a form of marketing where you identify a firm that has a product to sell, and then do it for them. The essence of affiliate marketing is that you get it done online, through the use of technologies such as banners that you can place on a website or blog you own. You can also use email marketing as well as the use of social media to get the job done as well.

Making money using affiliate marketing involves receiving a commission for every sale you make. The typical commissions usually differ from one firm to another. In addition to that, there are many affiliate marketing firms that offer bonuses if you reach or exceed a certain target.

What Niches Are

When you start doing affiliate marketing, you will come across the term niche' a lot. Basically, a niche is the subset of people you will be marketing to most of the time, or the industry you will choose to work in. Once you have made up your mind to do affiliate marketing, the next step in the process would be to identify the niche that you would prefer to work in.

For instance, are you interested in selling products and services that would appeal to people in the financial world, or are you more interested in electronics or gaming? It's important that you try to find a perfect fit for yourself as early as possible. This will help you pick the best affiliate marketer to work with. Some will have multiple products that you can market for them, so being very clear about which products you want to deal with will also make it easier for you to choose which product lines to sell for them.

Choosing The Right Niche

It might not seem important at first, but choosing the best niche for yourself will go a long way in making your affiliate marketing venture more profitable. Choosing a niche that you know inside out will make it easier for you to market goods and services to people. For instance, if you are really good at gaming, it will be very easy for you to know what appeals to other gamers out there.

If you then choose to use a specific means of marketing such as email marketing or putting ads on a website, you will then be able to come up with a marketing strategy that will appeal to such individuals. For instance, if you want to start a blog on which you will place ads that will generate revenue for you, you will be in a much better position to figure out how to structure the blog and what information to include in it in order to attract more customers. The same goes for any other products such as cosmetics, books and even financial products.

In addition to that, you will find that if you choose to market something that you are passionate about, you are likely to find it easier and have more fun while at it. For instance, there are some people who love talking about and using makeup. If you want to be an affiliate marketing agent and are one such person, choosing to market cosmetics will just be doing something that you love and getting paid for it.

The other benefit of choosing one niche that you love rather than trying to do everything at once is that it makes you a lot more focused. You will be able to come up with marketing strategies that will work since you will have a singular goal. Multiple surveys done about affiliate marketing show that the people who focus on only one niche tend to be more effective and more successful than those who do not. This is therefore a strategy to make more.

In summary, if you are having some cash flow problems or simply want to make more, you should consider trying out affiliate marketing. You are unlikely to start making big bucks the moment you start marketing, but if you follow the above then you are likely to find it a relatively easy way to make a significant amount of money on the site. In fact, there are many people who end up quitting their regular jobs and focusing solely on affiliate marketing, since it pays well if done correctly.

THE 50 BEST AFFILIATE MARKETING NICHES IN 2024

1. Fitness Equipment
2. Organic and Natural Foods
3. Sustainable Living
4. Personal Finance and Investing
5. Home Office Furniture
6. Online Learning Courses
7. Beauty and Skincare Products
8. Pet Care and Accessories
9. Tech Gadgets and Accessories
10. Digital Marketing Tools
11. Outdoor Gear and Equipment
12. Travel Accessories
13. DIY and Home Improvement
14. Parenting and Baby Products
15. Sustainable Fashion
16. Weight Loss Programs
17. Vegan and Plant-Based Lifestyle
18. Gaming Accessories
19. Self-Help and Personal Development
20. Eco-Friendly Products
21. Subscription Boxes
22. Home Decor
23. Language Learning Resources
24. Remote Work Tools
25. Mobile Apps
26. Hobby Supplies (e.g., art, crafts)
27. Renewable Energy Solutions
28. Gadgets for Remote Work

29. Virtual Reality Products
30. Smart Home Devices
31. Educational Toys for Kids
32. Niche Diets (e.g., keto, paleo)
33. DIY Beauty Products
34. Kitchen Gadgets
35. Outdoor Hobbies (e.g., gardening, birdwatching)
36. Water Sports Equipment
37. Sustainable Gardening
38. Specialty Coffee and Tea
39. Personal Safety Products
40. Survivalist Gear
41. Sustainable Cleaning Products
42. Minimalist Living
43. Mental Health Resources
44. Sports Nutrition
45. E-learning Platforms
46. DIY Tech Projects
47. Language Translation Tools
48. Eco-Friendly Cleaning
49. Smart Home Security Systems
50. Health & Wellness Products

Chapter 2

How To Locate Great Affiliate Offers

Once you decide to start making money using affiliate marketing, the next step would be to try and identify an offer that will turn out to be profitable for you. One of the classical mistakes that many people make when venturing into the world of affiliate marketing is simply signing on to one marketing program without first finding out what's available for them, or figuring out if it's actually a good program. Remember, once you join a particular program, you might need to put a significant amount of effort in the program before seeing the kinds of returns that many people get when they start affiliate marketing. Finding that the program is just not for you after you have worked at it so hard can be discouraging.

To avoid this, you should always make an effort to be patient. Biding your time and finding out as much as you can about a particular program before joining it is essential to ensuring that you will be satisfied with it in the long term. Some of the things you might need to do to identify a high quality one include:

Find Out The Terms Of Payment

You should not join any affiliate offer until you are sure about how you will be paid. You should always make sure that you choose programs that have a payment system that you are comfortable with. If not, you should consider negotiating with the administrators for different terms, though this might not always work.

Some of the things that you need to check when doing this include making sure that the mode of payment is agreeable to you, and that they also pay at intervals that you are satisfied with. One thing you ought to check is the minimum amount of money that is paid out. If it turns out that the minimum is too high, it means that you might wait for longer before getting your first paycheck. If you are not comfortable with this, you might as well avoid it.

Make sure you are comfortable with the niches offered

There are some affiliate programs that offer multiple niches, which means that you only need to sign up and then promote what you are comfortable with. Others are very specific, providing goods and services of a very specific nature.

Before joining an affiliate program, it's always wise to find out what you will be marketing, and then making sure that you are comfortable marketing this niche. Even if the rest of the terms are excellent but it turns out that the products or services are out of your comfort zone, you should be careful about signing up for such an offer. You might just end up having a hard time promoting the goods or services simply because you are not familiar with them or do not have that much interest in them.

Don't forget to go through the terms and conditions

When you spot such an offer, it would be wise for you to pore through the terms and conditions. This will give you an excellent idea of whether it's a high quality deal or not. Most people shy away from doing this since it's thought that the terms are usually too wordy. However, doing so will help you avoid any future regrets and frustrations, particularly if it turns out that the terms are not very friendly.

What are other people saying?

Though it's not always possible to do so, you should try to get some feedback from some people who have come into contact with such a deal. For instance, if you go online, you can find tons of reviews on many different kinds of offers, and you can then use this to figure out whether the one you are thinking of joining is good enough or not.

Most high quality deals will have many positive reviews, and some of these reviews can even have information on how the deals work. You should also expect a few negative reviews for each of the programs even if they are not that bad. This simply means that coming across one negative review should not stop you from buying the product; you should always try to get the bigger picture.

Find out more about the metrics

Once you sign up for the program, how will you know when a sale has been made from your strategy? How do you keep tabs of things such as click through rates if they are applicable? Do you have access to any statistical information that can help you optimize your marketing strategy? A killer marketing offer will have facilities to help you do all of these, which in turn makes monitoring of your marketing much easier. You should therefore always try to find out if the firm offering the deal has such services, and even try them out if you can.

The most important thing to remember is that when doing affiliate marketing, you should always try to get involved in a program that you are sure will work for rather than against you. This calls for patience and an analysis of the above details before making the decision.

Chapter 3

4 Tools To Build Your Website

As unbelievable as this may sound, it's utterly practical and very much happening today. "The Majority of Small Business Owners Don't have Websites." Websites to some may seem like a joke but on a very serious note, it's a serious business on its own; and one of the most present fundamentally essential tools for business. We will all concur that we are living in a surprisingly dynamic digital age where almost everything relies on internet and electronic devices.

Just to highlight a few benefits of owning a website a business owner regardless of the magnitude of your business; to start with, it's the most presently available and effective platform through which one can showcase their proficiency, services and products; in simple words, in addition to owning a platform through which you can use to achieve this, you will be marketing your products and services at the same time. Other advantages of owning a website include; interaction with prospect clients, creating a team of loyalists, to mention but a few. To sum it up, owning a website makes your entire venture look professional.

If asked why they do not own a website, many people like to blame it on the inability to create one due to the supposedly complex coding involved and the incapacity to hire a professional website designer. Good news is that you can now create a website without necessarily knowing how to code credit to the universally available tools. In this article, we will be discussing in details about precisely four simple tools that can be used to create a website; including why we chose it, what it costs and why you should use it.

1. Yola

Yola actually lets you build a simple website by filling out a few straightforward forms after picking a template. One starts by creating a rough outline and then using an in-place editing tool, smoothen out the entire site. Unlike other website creating tools, Yola actually lets you really dig into your web until the desired effect is attained. Also be interested to know that with Yola, you can easily integrate a number of impressive third party services such PayPal and Google Maps into your site. If you like being using graphic and photos, then you can effortlessly use Flickr and

Ribbet to achieve this.

What it Costs - The lowest and the very basic web-designing tool and a Yola.com address are positively free. However, for extra features; ones with somewhat better looking templates and liberal ability to use you own customized domain, it will cost you about $100 per year for this upgrade.

Bottom Line - Supposing you are after a professional site, and one that is basic; at a very reasonable cost, then Yola is actually the tool for you.

2. Jimdo

In simple, illustrative words possible, Jimdo can be described as "a free simple website building tool that does what any respectable website builder can and ought to do." Kindly note that, to enjoy a better experience with Jimdo, an upgrade is advised which by the way costs a few dollars and unlocks some of the cool business features such as page-view stats, newsletters, password-protected employee-only pages and PayPal, to mention but a few.

Jimdo's Current Cost-like Yola, the basic features and Jimdo.com address is totally freely. However, there are other paid versions; Jimdo Pro which costs $5 per month and Jimdo Business which costs $15 per month. The latter features online selling and unlimited data storage, two domain names and importantly, Business-Specific site templates. With the pro and business version, you have the liberty to advertise anything you feel like and in any way you please and therefore you can use your website for affiliate marketing

Bottom line - To emphasize what we stated earlier, the free version of this tool isn't actually worth your time. All you will get from its free version is basic, but somewhat enthralling templates. For super and quite satisfying experience, consider an upgrade. In summary, Jimdo is best for individuals interested in a simple yet functional website with a professional touch.

3. Wix

Wix is yet another simple website building tool that is actually easy to use and doesn't necessarily need any knowledge in programming. Unfortunately, given that it runs on adobe flash, it can only be supported (run) on PC's but not on most mobile devices; even worse, including all Apple (Ios powered) iPads.

Assuming that you don't mind about this fact; the definitely Wix is an ideal website building tool for you. Forget about its downsides, Wix strength lies on the fact that it occasions you with the liberty to create a rather elegant looking and professional yet efficient website that can take care of all your business needs. Be interested to know that Wix is also integrated with a sufficiently powerful image editing tool that lets you edit all your photos and images at ago.

Wix's Current Cost-like all the other website building tools we've discussed in this article, Wix's basic version and Wix.com address is absolutely free. However, there are paid versions which costs between $5 and $16 per month depending on the features you intend to subscribe to. Finally, and importantly, with the paid version Wix tool, you have the liberty to venture into money generating activities such as Affiliate Marketing, advertising and such.

Verdict - for all artistic natured individuals, positively fascinated by not only elegant looking site but also professionally built and fully functional one, then definitely this is the tool to use.

4. LaunchRock

Unlike with the other website building tools we've discussed in this article, LaunchRock (launchrock.com) technically provides you with a platform through which you can build a somewhat sophisticated website; one you can use to, among other things market your services and outsource marketing services through marketing programs such as Affiliate Marketing. In addition, thanks to its newsletter feature, you can woo a number of loyal followers; most of which you can convert into prospective clients.

What it cost – Launchrock.com is positively free and unlike other presently available website building tools, allows one to incorporate paid premium add-ons into their site.

Bottom line – Launchrock.com, given that it already has a substantial user base is definitely ideal for all business owners interested in making progress as far as their business is concerned.

Conclusion

Kindly note that this 4 website building tools aren't the only available in the market; actually, there is a plethora of them. It's therefore upon you depending on the specific goals you intend to achieve to choose what suits your needs. Finally, once you've successfully launched your site don't forget to follow the simple SEO to make it in the online market, acquire some knowledge in trending issues such as internet marketing and their relevancy to today's business world. As a reminder, and a necessity, you can start with simple marketing techniques such as affiliate marketing, and always be on the lookout for any update.

Chapter 4

Writing High-Converting Pages

One of the commonest ways in which affiliate marketing is done is by setting up a web page, making sure that it has enough traffic and then putting ads and other offers on the page. The goal is to ensure that the people who visit the page will then click the ads and then buy the goods you are marketing, for which you will get a commission. For most people, setting up the page and signing up for an affiliate marketing program is the easy part. The hard part is to get enough traffic that has the interest to buy whatever is being sold on the site. The only way to make this happen is by developing a systematic method of setting up the website, so that it's optimized to encourage people to convert into buyers. Some of the elements you might need to include in such a page to facilitate this include:

The Headline

The headline on the page is one of the most important elements, since it will determine whether you interest people long enough to keep reading and buy what you have to offer or not. It's important to remember that over the past few years, most people's attention span has reduced. This is in part due to the fact that they are exposed to too much information, and this in turn means that they have to be very selective.

To ensure that the page you set up has a high conversion rate, you need to get an attention grabbing headline. Someone should be able to look at it and decide within seconds that it's worth their time, so that they can keep reading it. This also means that it should be short enough (preferably less than 20 words long) so that someone can get the gist of it with a single glance. Another trick you can use is to combine the headline with a relevant image. For instance, if you are running an affiliate programming strategy where you sell phones, having a phone manufacturer logo next to the headline might make it more noticeable to people who are interested in it, and who will therefore most likely buy what you have to offer.

The Use Of Images

They say a picture speaks a thousand words, and this is never truer than in marketing. People are more likely to be responsive to a page if it has images that are relevant to what is being offered. However, there are things you might need to keep in mind to make such images useful. For one, they should fit the page properly; images that look visibly sloppy tend to make the whole site unprofessional and will make people not take it seriously. The images should also be of high quality. You should particularly avoid pictures whose resolution is not correct, or those which are obviously stock photos. If you can, pay for high quality pictures from a photographer.

To have the best effect, the images should work seamlessly with the design of the site. Having photos which seem to clash with the rest of the site should be avoided. It's also wise to ensure that you don't overdo it; having too many photos on one page is just as bad as not having any photos as well.

An Adequate Explanation

The headline has attracted a potential customer, the subhead line has made them stay and the images have interested them to try and find out more about what the site has to offer. Why should the potential customer buy what you have to offer? You will always need to provide an explanation as to why the customer needs the service or product you are offering, or why they should buy from you rather than from anyone else. Tips to make this work include making sure that you put yourself in the position of the customer, and then try to write the explanation from their point of view.

A common mistake that many people make when trying to sell goods or services using affiliate marketing is having long winded stories and explanations. However, the fact that so many of such pages exist means that if a customer has to scroll down past a long story about your experience with the product or other literature, you are likely to lose them. Always try to be succinct enough. Try to send one short, clear message that will appeal to the customer.

Provide Contact Information

Always provide some contact information within the page so as to encourage people to contact you should they need further clarification. Making sure that the contact information looks professional (such as by using a custom domain name, rather than the free ones) will give an air of professionalism. The potential customers are more likely to trust you in such cases.

These are just some of the basic issues you need to take note of to come up with a high converting affiliate marketing page. Always consider seeking help from an affiliate marketing consultant to help you set one up, particularly if you are doing this for the first time.

Chapter 5

Building Quality Back-links To Your Site

When you are interested in doing affiliate marketing, one of the most important things you will need to do is ensure that the page of the site from which the offers are provided is popular. Remember, you will need to have a large number of people visit the site, find out what you have to offer and then buy some of the goods and services that are present there. Considering the fact that most people look for information using social media, it therefore stands to reason that by simply making your site have a high page rank, you can achieve this with ease.

There are many ways to do this, but one of the most effective is through the use of back-links. These are links from other sites to yours, and which will direct people to your website. The presence of such back-links performs a number of functions. For one, it makes it possible to have people shuttled from the other pages to yours by clicking the links, thus increasing the number of visitors in the site. In addition to that, having a large number of back-links on a site also helps to increase its page rank, which ultimately leads to more traffic.

What should be your goals when getting people to the site?

If you are interested in increasing the traffic to any website, it would be important to have a few ground rules to follow. These are not mandatory; you only need them to guide you in making the decision on how to improve this traffic. One of the most important of these is making sure that you prioritize quality over quantity. The people who are directed to the site should be interested in buying what you have to offer, rather than just simply visiting the site and then logging off.

With this in mind, you will then find it much easier to decide on how and where to get the back-links to the site from.

What are the characteristics of a high quality back link?

For you to ensure that the back-links attracts traffic with high conversion rates, one of the first things they will need to be is relevant. For instance, if you somehow manage to have your link in another site, you should make sure that it is somehow related to the type of campaign you are running.

A good example of this is when you sell cosmetics through

the affiliate marketing program. In this case, it would be wise to have a back-link that originates from a site with similar interests. You would also need to make sure that the word or phrase that is attached to the back link has some relevance. This means that choosing a random word for this should not be tolerated.

The other thing you need to watch out for is the quality of the site from which the link is originating. Most of the time, links that bring in traffic that converts quickly tend to be from sites with a good reputation. Once again, this is an instance where you should always go for quality over quantity. You would rather have a few back-links from a site with a high page rank and which has engrossing content, rather than a large number of links from sites that are not of high quality.

Some of the ways to get back-links

The essence of getting back-links is by identifying a site that is similar to yours, and then requesting for them to link to you. There are several ways of doing this. One of these is through a link exchange program, where you agree to exchange the back links. Another way to do this would be through the use of guest blogging.

For instance, if you find a blog that has something to do with what you sell, you could offer to write a post on behalf of the blogger. This is normally welcomed since it introduces some fresh content on the site, and relieves the owner of having to write the post for that time. When doing this, you can include a link to your blog or site. For this to be effective, you would need to first ask permission to link to your site, and also make sure that the content is of high quality so that people will be keen to learn more. You should also make sure that the blog you are guest blogging for is of high quality and popular.

In addition to the above, social media has also become a great way for back linking, given the huge popularity of such sites.

The Importance Of Monitoring

You should always make sure that you monitor the state of the back linking to your site. There are some online applications that you can use to do this. Remember, just because you have established the link does not mean that it will be present forever.

In summary, the use of back-links is a very potent way to boost the popularity of the affiliate marketing site, which will in turn increase sales from it.

Chapter 6

How To Expand Your Web Traffic

The Topic about Website Traffic in entirety is quite broad and can't be covered in a simple and not even long than 200 pages Book. For those of you who own blogs and websites, you will completely agree with me that traffic is actually the fuel that drives on the path of success. Without traffic, all your ventures are utterly futile. As we all know, of all the sources of traffic, search engine traffic rocks and it shouldn't even subtly surprise you that it's the most sought after source of traffic, what's more, it's absolutely free. In this article, we will be discussing a number of ways through which you can diversify your search engine traffic, but first, let's start with the basic.

What does it mean by "Expanding your Website Traffic?"

When we talk about "expanding your website traffic" we simply refer to the act of generating/getting traffic from as many different sources you can succeed to amass. The question many of you may be asking yourself is "why get traffic from as many different sources?" to answer your question, I would like to first explain one very important aspect in relation to search engine traffic.

Truth be told, Google is actually a Giant and if not everyone, at least 97% of internet users use Google when searching for online content. Google being a key player, in order to run efficiently, it's rudely known to come up with this not so encouraging updates that often tend to hurt even those of "US" who have perfected the art of blogging and use the whitest/clean method of driving traffic to our sites. The sad thing is that no one actually knows when the next Google update is going to be employed and what it's going to be. So literally, website owners are living in fear of the unknown.

Back to our theme topic, when you diversify your website traffic, you ought not to worry about any of the regular Google's updates. At worst, if by bad luck you get hurt by any of their updates, it won't be that severe. The following, about 6 tips are actually going to help you stay safe from Google's update:

1. Always remember that Google isn't actually the only search engine.

Be reminded that there is Bing and Yahoo, and they are much alive and also quite significant. To get the most out of search engines, learn basic SEO techniques such as back-linking, content creation. Most importantly, learn to stick clean methods of traffic creation.

2. Get on Google+

According to studies, it's been claimed that having an account with Google plus literally means setting up authorship with Google and consequently boosts your traffic rating with Google. In addition, it also helps when it comes to business listing. Finally, given that Google plus is a social platform, it can be used to channel traffic into your site. In addition, unlike other social sites, Google plus looks more businesslike and can unapologetically be used in marketing. Finally, followers gained from Google plus won't feel bored or disrupted should you decide to venture into affiliate marketing.

3. When creating Content, try as much as possible to optimize to look like you Homepage

It's a known fact that many of website owners always give their best shot when creating their site's homepage. Mainly because (which is actually true) they heard that a landing page has to be flawless and professionally created. Therefore, the same effort invested when creating Homepage should also be employed when creating other contents. What's more, when creating links, you should stick to the "deep link" building culture whereby your links are not only confined to homepages alone.

4. You've heard this before, but I will say it again, "Get Social"

By getting social, am not referring to the nowadays common trend of creating account with all the existing social platforms. You have to get your priorities right and decide where to invest your time. Many success stories have been attributed to people's ability to get social. If for instance you choose Facebook and twitter as your main social site, learn everything you can be able to about them and try to your level best to do your best to the best of your ability. Furthermore, be advised to always drive organic traffic by sticking to proven traffic generating methods. Incorporate these Social media add-ons in your main site and keep referring your main site in your social platform; consider posting your sites links in your social platform.

5. Build and maintain a newsletter

Forget about what you may have heard there about email marketing. Email marketing is still and will be for a long time be a king. When building a newsletter, your main objective should be to get as many email address as possible. Sending frequent updates to your subscribed followers will ensure that you maintain constant flow of traffic. In addition, also note that you can actually convert this into being a source through which you let your followers know of all progress you are making. Finally, don't forget to use it to your advantage after generating enough traffic to create diverse money generating sources in your website among them being affiliate marketing.

6. Diversify your links

Finally, and as a reiteration to what has already been discussed, learn to diversify you links. This greatly reduces risks. Aim at building links with a number of directories, press releases and blogs. Being diversified often makes the whole process look natural before real people's eyes and search engine robotics.

Chapter 7

Scaling Your Affiliate Site Like A Pro

Suppose you have joined an affiliate marketing program, and are finally starting to see some progress in the form of regular earnings from your campaigns. What next? One of the problems many people run into at this point is developing a sense of complacency, and getting the same returns over and over. However, you should remember that when you are doing affiliate marketing, the only thing that limits how much you can earn is how much effort you put into the process and how creative you are. In fact, if you are persistent enough at finding the right marketing formula, you are very likely to make affiliate marketing the source of most of your monthly earnings.

For this to happen, however, you will need to consistently scale your marketing program. This means finding new sources of revenue, and also optimizing the ones that you have to make them even more profitable. Some of the things you might need to do in order to make this happen include:

Have some form of tracking system in place

One of the worst strategies you can adopt when doing affiliate marketing is doing it without having to refer to any metrics. It is important that you always try to find out how your campaign is doing, and where the most revenue comes from. This can only be done by using tracking software that will give you information about click through rates, cost per view and even give you a diagram of where the most clicks come from. For instance, if you use both email marketing and a website to do the affiliate marketing, you might find that one of your sites does better than the other. The only way to know this and then optimize the income from that site is if you have the tracking software.

These days, a large number of affiliate marketing programs will also give you tracking solutions once you open an affiliate account with them. Even if they do not, you can also subscribe to third party solutions such as Prosper202 to get this information.

Have A Landing Page

Having a landing page is an easy way to increase the returns on your marketing campaign and build your email list. You can use the landing page to provide more information about the product or service you are marketing. This goes a long way in convincing people to buy what you have to offer, particularly if the landing page is well made.

Email Opt-In Headliners That Convert:

In my experience helping people avoid a negative situation converts better than leading them to success. For example, if someone spills coffee on themselves strangers will be more than willing to help. However, if someone states they can get you xyz results in 30 days, people immediately thing, "scam." Always use psychology to your advantage so if you are marketing to cold traffic always use a headline that helps them avoid pain. After they opt into your email list it's is okay to use positive headlines for your emails etc.

EXAMPLE #1. RESULTS FOCUS

The 5 Step Blueprint To (RESULTS) [QUICKLY] (WITHOUT THINGS THEY HATE)

Include 3-4 bullet points refuting any objections and have the email opt in with a button that says, "DOWNLOAD"

EXAMPLE: "The 5 Step Blueprint To Landing Your Dream Job In

30 Days Without A College Degree."

EXAMPLE #2. RESULTS FOCUS

How To Get (RESULTS) [QUICKLY] (WITHOUT THINGS

THEY HATE)

Include 3-4 bullet points refuting any objections and have the email

opt in with a button that says, "DOWNLOAD"

EXAMPLE: "How to Get Out of Debt in 30 Days or Less With This Step By Step Framework"

EXAMPLE #3. ACTION FOCUS

What To Do If (HOT BUTTON)

Include 3-4 bullet points refuting any objections and have the email

opt in with a button that says, "DOWNLOAD"

EXAMPLE: "What To Do If Your Husband Is Looking At Other Women"

EXAMPLE #4. CUSTOMER FOCUS

The 3 Biggest Mistakes (IDEAL CUSTOMER) Makes (CAUSING

THIS PROBLEM)

Include 3-4 bullet points refuting any objections and have the email

opt in with a button that says, "DOWNLOAD"

EXAMPLE: "The 3 Biggest Mistakes You Make That Keep You Poor"

EXAMPLE #5. APPROACH FOCUS

Why (COMMON SENSE APPROACH) Doesn't Work (AND

WHAT TO DO ABOUT IT)

Include 3-4 bullet points refuting any objections and have the email

opt in with a button that says, "DOWNLOAD"

EXAMPLE: "Why Most Online Businesses Fail And What To Do
About It"

Consider Doing Marketing In Related Niches

It's always a good idea to focus on one particular niche,

which allows you to specialize in that specific niche. However,

there are times when two niches might be related to each other, and

you could opt to get involved in both. For instance, if you do

affiliate marketing for a firm that sells literature on how to gain

weight, you could find another marketer who provides supplements

and then market them both. These are products that are

complementary, and people who buy one are likely to buy the

other. This way, you will help people more and make more money

out of it.

Get Traffic From More Than One Site

You will need internet traffic to make sales. When you have just started out the affiliate marketing program, chances are that you will focus on building traffic from only a small number of sources, such to your website or blog. As time goes by, you should consider getting more traffic from other sources. For instance, you could try using social media to get some of the traffic, as well as guest blogging on more sites so that you can back-link to yours.

Consider Using Custom Ad Banners

When doing affiliate marketing, you will often get banner codes from the affiliate program and then put them on your site. However, there are many times when this might not work at all. The commonest problem you will encounter is finding that the ads are tacky, and make your site look cheap. To avoid this, you should consider designing ads that are consistent with the product or service you are marketing, but which are also suited to fit your site as well.

There are some online services that can be used for this, but if you are creative enough you can make the ad banners on your own. If you are new to this, you could try to learn about online ad design and then use the principles you have learnt to come up with them.

Consult Other Sources

A great way to scale your affiliate marketing program and make more from it is by consulting. For instance, you could identify a high quality online marketing firm, and then have them evaluate your program. When this is done professionally, you will easily identify the weak spots that you can improve on, and also get feedback on how to make your program more successful. The fact that this information is usually very specific to individual settings means that it is often very valuable. Of course, you would need to work with a very good consultant to achieve this.

Chapter 8

Affiliate Marketing 30 Day Challenge

Lets' face it! Besides providing solution to people's problems, we are all interested in making extra cash from our online ventures. When it comes to blogging, there are actually a myriad ways through which one can make money. However, and on a very serious note, of all the presently existing money making schemes, affiliate marketing is preferably the most common and supremely the easiest of all. But how well are you familiar with "Affiliate Marketing?" Under this segment we will be discussing about Affiliate marketing in details; explaining everything every affiliate marketer need to know, concluding with a very critical subject of "making affiliate marketing a 30 day challenge."

What is Affiliate Marketing?

Before defining affiliate marketing, let me first refresh our minds! I presume that we all know two ways through which one can make money online. They essentially constitute:

1. Selling your own stuff.

2. Selling or promoting someone else's stuff, in turn getting

paid for it.

In this section however, we will be expounding on the second method. For those interested in selling their own stuff, consider starting with a Book (but that's another topic on its own, and one for another day).

In this section, I will be defining affiliate marketing using 6 simple methods.

1. To begin with, to be an affiliate marketer, you first ought to have a blog or a website.

2. The second step will be to identify a product or service that you can confidently sell to your followers (readers). This basically involves understanding your readers and the niche you are advocating for then partnering with the company that sells/provides the product or service you intend to market.

3. You will then, by your own means market this product or service for the company.

4. For instance, you will be charged with alerting your readers of the great product or service company X provides/offers, by either writing about it or placing a banner or button somewhere in your

site.

5. It's through these links that your reader will be directed to the company's website, being provided with an opportunity to purchase that service or product.

6. Should they decide to purchase the product or service, company X will be able to see that that specific buyer was referred by you and they will then award you with a commission as a way of showing gratitude.

6 Laws Every Blogger Ought to Know About Affiliate Marketing

As easy as affiliate marketing may sound, to truly succeed, one needs to be tirelessly committed and fully aware of the code of ethics they ought to abide by. We will be going through six laws that ought to be observed in order for one to increase their affiliate earnings. They are as follows:

1. Feed People with the Information they Really Want - Regardless of whether you started a blog or website to quench your writing hobby or for commercial purposes, to thrive as an affiliate marketer, you will be required to build a group of loyal followers

who can buy whatever item you recommend. To achieve this, you should work to "be known" as a person, by regularly releasing incredible content. Posting authentic content drives people to trust you, in turn making them try whatever idea you throw their way.

2. Make it a Habit to Market Products you use or intimately know - You should all know that, people are really intelligent and most of them have a sixth sense that lets them know whether someone is in business to help them or is just interested in making money. One thumb of rule when choosing a product to market is, "if you can't find something good to talk about a product or service, don't even thing about marketing it."

3. Become an Evangelist of your Chosen Product and persistently spread its gospel to your readers - Keep telling people everything including both the good and the bad about the product you are marketing with utmost honesty. Remember, your work is only to market, let them decide on their own whether to purchase it or not.

4. Build and Email List and Keep updating your readers of every development you find about product - Building an email list will help you gain and keep readers. As a marketer, you should know

that it's from loyal followers that one can be able to find prospective clients. Most importantly, you should learn to attend to all questions that you are asked through email.

5. It's a Hard Fact! There is no such thing as Overnight Success-the trick to blogging as a marketer is momentum. Note that when starting out, you may not be able to earn anything. Keep playing along and allow your consistence and determination to pay you in due time.

6. Always know the terms and conditions of service you are trying to market.

Affiliate Marketing 30 Day Challenge

It is obvious that affiliate marketing is quite a broad topic and if ventured in, a demanding task. Therefore, it's not something that you will wake up one morning and do in a click. You need to have strategic plans through which you can achieve this. The main aim of this Topic is to light your path into the journey of affiliate marketing. Now the great task is upon you, depending on your schedule, come up with things you indent to do in Precisely 30 days. Start with the basics like creating a website, creating content, investing in SEO, choosing an affiliate marketing platform and such. Remember, all this has to be done in 30 days, so take your time and see your efforts paying off.

Chapter 9

Final Thoughts

In summary, I would like to reiterate what I said earlier, "Affiliate marketing can be, and is always overwhelming" especially if you don't know the key/principle elements to becoming successful. On the other hand, it can be quite easy once you are aware of the "tips" (secrets) other successful affiliate marketers use. Basically, affiliate marketing success entirely relies upon three key factors:

Visitors/Traffic - We are now aware that in order to make money through affiliate marketing, one need to convert visitors to paying customers for your merchant associate(s). It's therefore needless to say that the more visitors one has, the more his/her chances of converting a substantial amount of visitors to the merchants site. Building a substantial and consistent flow of traffic isn't that easy but it's much practical. During your free time, research about SEO and master how to do it.

Click Rate - Your success will also depend on the number of clicks your visitors make. Note that throwing up banners and posters "carelessly" in your site will appear disruptive and may even cost you a number of followers. Be orderly and arrange things in an organized manner. The more presentable your work looks the more professional you appear. If your work appears professional before your readers, you will have an easy time convincing them that the product you are advocating for is indeed reliable and of good quality.

Conversion Rate - This is where the money is. Remember, you only get commissions once someone purchases the product. Many affiliate marketers often leave the visitor to decide for themselves (which is a profoundly good thing), but you have to show your stand. Don't force your readers to purchase the product, give your opinion/verdict and let them pick up from there.

Practice everything you have learned in this Book. Also remember that patience does really pay when it comes to affiliate marketing. As mentioned before, it may take time before you see any progress, if you keep doing what is right, definitely, in due time, you will be reaping BIG. Finally, always be smart and learn to observe opportunities from a far.